DISASTER SCIENCE

THE SCIENCE OF A HURRICANE

MARY REINA

CHERRY LAKE
Publishing

Published in the United States of America by Cherry Lake Publishing
Ann Arbor, Michigan
www.cherrylakepublishing.com

Consultants: Jennifer Rivers Cole, Department of Earth and Planetary Sciences, Harvard University;
Marla Conn, ReadAbility, Inc.
Editorial direction: Red Line Editorial
Book design and illustration: Design Lab

Photo Credits: Shutterstock Images, cover, 1; David J. Phillip/AP Images, 5, 25; NASA, 7, 12, 18; NASA/Corbis, 9; John
Plumber/DK Images, 11; Corbis, 15; Charles Sykes/AP Images, 21; US Army, 26; Sayre Berman/Corbis, 28

Library of Congress Cataloging-in-Publication Data
    Reina, Mary, author.
    The science of a hurricane / by Mary Reina.
        pages cm. -- (Disaster science)
    Audience: 11.
    Audience: Grade 4 to 6.
    Includes bibliographical references and index.
    ISBN 978-1-63137-624-5 (hardcover) -- ISBN 978-1-63137-669-6 (pbk.) -- ISBN 978-1-63137-714-3 (pdf ebook) --
ISBN 978-1-63137-759-4 (hosted ebook)
    1. Hurricanes--Juvenile literature. I. Title.
    QC944.2.R45 2015
    551.55'2--dc23   2014004030

Cherry Lake Publishing would like to acknowledge the work of
The Partnership for 21st Century Skills. Please visit www.p21.org
for more information.

Printed in the United States of America
Corporate Graphics Inc.
July 2014

ABOUT THE AUTHOR

Mary Reina is an experienced science and nature writer specializing in books and articles for
elementary school readers. Her work includes two books and more than 50 articles covering various
aspects of science, history, nature, the environment, and astronomy.

TABLE OF CONTENTS

THE FIERCEST STORMS ON EARTH

Hurricanes are the world's largest, most destructive storms. Their swirling masses of wind and water destroy cities, take lives, and can leave thousands without homes. One of the worst hurricanes in recent history hit the United States on August 29, 2005. Hurricane Katrina killed more than 1,800 people in Mississippi and Louisiana and caused more than $108 billion in damage. No other hurricane in the nation's history has been as costly.

[21ST CENTURY SKILLS LIBRARY]

Hurricane Katrina left much of New Orleans, Louisiana, under water.

Hurricanes that form in the Atlantic Ocean, the Northeast Pacific, and the Gulf of Mexico hit the United States, Mexico, and the Caribbean islands. The hurricane season in these areas lasts from June 1 until November 30. Hurricanes also hit Asia, Australia, and Africa. They are often known as typhoons or cyclones in these areas, but they are the same type of storm. The hurricane season is different in each area. For instance, Australia's hurricane season lasts from November to April. Scientists group hurricanes, typhoons, and cyclones under the term *tropical cyclone.*

NAMING HURRICANES

The World Meteorological Organization (WMO) names hurricanes to avoid confusion when two or more form in the same area. The names also make it easier to inform the public about a particular storm. The names come from an alphabetical list maintained by the WMO. When a storm is so deadly or costly that its name seems inappropriate for future use, the name is removed from the list. Katrina's spot on the list was taken over by the name Karen.

Tropical cyclones are rotating systems of clouds and thunderstorms. Each one begins as a loose collection of storms. If this stormy weather stays intact for at least 24 hours, it is called a tropical disturbance. As wind speeds increase, the storm begins to rotate. When its wind speeds range between 23 and 38 miles per hour (37 and 61 kmh), the system is called a tropical depression.

A tropical depression becomes a tropical storm when its wind speeds range between 39 and 73 miles per hour (63 and 117 kmh). At that point, the storm is given a

[21ST CENTURY SKILLS LIBRARY]

name. On August 24, 2005, tropical storm Katrina moved through the Bahamas. On August 25, its wind speeds reached at least 74 miles per hour (119 kmh), officially making it a hurricane. Hurricane Katrina then made its way toward the United States. On August 29, it hit Louisiana with winds speeds of 127 miles per hour (204 kmh). In a matter of days, it had transformed from a small storm into a devastating system of swirling wind.

Hurricanes are big enough to be seen from space.

HURRICANE FORMATION

Hurricanes form around low-pressure systems. These are areas where air pressure is lower than the pressure of the surrounding atmosphere. A low-pressure system develops when warm, moist air rises into the atmosphere. As the warm air rises, it cools, **condenses** into tiny droplets of water, and sometimes produces a thunderstorm.

Occasionally, if several of these thunderstorms are near each other, they come together. This storm system

Hurricanes form more easily in warmer water,
shown here in red, orange, and yellow.

may turn into a hurricane, or it may simply **dissipate**.
Certain conditions must be in place for the storm system
to progress from a tropical depression to a tropical storm
and finally to a hurricane. First, the system must develop
over water that is at least 80 degrees Fahrenheit (26°C).
The ocean water evaporates and creates warm, moisture-
filled air. Next, light winds from different directions must

be present near the ocean surface. They come together and force the warm air upward. Now there is less air left at the surface. Cooler air rushes in to replace it. This air warms and rises, too. Higher in the atmosphere, the **humid** air cools, creating more clouds and thunderstorms. Some of the cooler air is pushed out over the storm and sinks back down. It picks up warmth and moisture from the ocean and rises again. The cluster of storms grows bigger and stronger. It begins to spin around its low-pressure system.

TROPICAL CYCLONE SIZE

Tropical cyclones average about 400 miles (640 km) across, but their size varies widely. Typhoon Tip hit Japan on October 12, 1979. It measured about 1,350 miles (2,170 km) across, making it the largest tropical cyclone on record. Tropical Storm Marco was among the smallest. It was just 23 miles (37 km) wide when it struck Mexico on October 7, 2008.

Sometimes multiple storm systems can form in the same region at the same time.

Because Earth rotates, the rushing air of the storm curves in a certain direction. This is known as the Coriolis effect. It gives a tropical cyclone its spinning motion. A storm north of the equator spins in a counterclockwise direction. Storms south of the equator spin in a clockwise direction.

As long as nothing breaks the cycle, the storm will act like a giant engine powered by heat. It will suck warmth out of the ocean and use it to grow bigger and stronger. Hurricanes begin to dissipate when they move over land or reach areas of cooler water. Without warm water to fuel them, they soon lose strength.

WIND IN A HURRICANE

This diagram shows how winds move as a hurricane forms. Based on this graphic and what you read about the conditions that lead to hurricanes, why do you think these storms form in the areas they do?

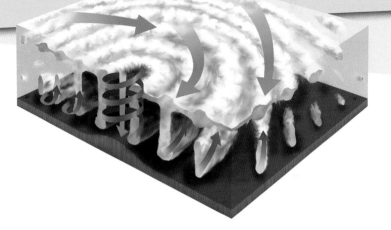

A Self-Feeding Machine

A hurricane draws its power from the energy provided by warm ocean water. At the center of a hurricane is a relatively calm area called the **eye**. Surrounding the eye is an area called the **eyewall**. This is the part of the hurricane containing the strongest winds and heaviest thunderstorms. It is formed as warm air rushes inward and turns upward into the storm. Finally, **rainbands** whirl around the entire structure like giant pinwheels. Together, each of these structures plays its own role in keeping the storm intact.

In the eye and around the rainbands, air from higher in the atmosphere sinks toward the surface. Sinking air warms and dries, creating a mostly cloud-free, rain-free eye. Meanwhile, low pressure at the ocean surface pulls in air from the surrounding area. This warm, moist air swirls into the eyewall and rainbands. The warm air rises and cools. Its water vapor condenses into rain. This process releases tremendous amounts of heat. Wind speeds increase, pulling more moisture into the storm. This creates more heat and further increases wind speed.

CHAPTER 3

TRACKING AND PREDICTING

In the early 1900s, people living in hurricane-prone areas did not know when hurricanes were coming toward them. Hurricane tracking was nothing like it is now. Meteorologists typically received information about storms at sea when ships came into port. Weather offices kept in touch with each other by telephone and **telegraph**. If telephone or telegraph lines broke down, so did communication. Tools such as **barometers**, **anemometers**, **rain gauges**, and thermometers were used to measure conditions as a hurricane approached land. However, these tools provided little advance warning of incoming storms, dramatically increasing the death toll. This fact is illustrated by the hurricane that hit Galveston, Texas, on September 8, 1900.

Huge parts of Galveston were completely destroyed by the 1900 hurricane.

Residents of Galveston were taken by surprise when the storm destroyed a long, wide area of their city. At least 6,000 of Galveston's approximately 40,000 people

SAFFIR-SIMPSON HURRICANE SCALE

This scale gives a 1 to 5 rating based on a hurricane's sustained wind speed. A Category 3 or above is considered a major hurricane.

Category	Wind Speed	Estimated Damage
1	74–95 miles per hour (119–153 kmh)	Dangerous winds; damage will occur
2	96–110 miles per hour (154–177 kmh)	Extremely dangerous winds; extensive damage will occur.
3	111–129 miles per hour (178–208 kmh)	Devastating damage will occur.
4	130–156 miles per hour (209–251 kmh)	Catastrophic damage will occur.
5	157+ miles per hour (252+ kmh)	Catastrophic damage will occur.

lost their lives. Thousands more from the surrounding area died as well. Such a terrible loss of life made this hurricane the deadliest ever to hit the United States.

Today, meteorologists use a huge collection of tools to track hurricanes. Some of the most important tools are the Geostationary Operational Environmental **Satellites** (GOES). They track storms and help scientists predict weather. The group of satellites circles Earth about 22,300 miles (35,900 km) above the surface. They move at the same speed the planet spins below them. This means that each satellite stays above a fixed point on Earth's surface. This gives the satellites the ability to monitor a particular area for any conditions that might trigger a hurricane.

Pilots called hurricane hunters fly special airplanes right into the eyes of hurricanes. The planes fly at a height of between 1,000 and 10,000 feet (305 and 3,050 m). Once they get the plane into the proper position, the pilots drop an instrument called a

GOES are large and contain several scientific instruments.

dropsonde into the hurricane. It measures a storm's wind speed, air pressure, and humidity.

Meteorologists on the ground interpret the information. Then they provide it to public officials and local news stations. People living in places where a hurricane is coming can prepare for the storm. Many people nail wooden boards over their windows to protect the glass. They can stock up on food, water, and medicine if they decide to stay in their homes. If the hurricane is predicted to be severe, people sometimes choose to leave the area. Governments may even order an **evacuation** to keep people safe.

THE FIRST FLIGHT INTO A HURRICANE

Hurricane hunting began on July 27, 1943. Colonel Joseph Duckworth and Lieutenant Ralph O'Hair of the US Army took an unplanned flight into a hurricane that hit the Texas coast. They braved the high winds, gathered information about the storm, and safely made it back to the base. Today, the men and women of the US Air Force's 53rd Weather Reconnaissance Squadron continue performing this dangerous job.

CHAPTER 4

ONE STORM, MANY DANGERS

Hurricane winds can rip an area apart in a matter of hours. Wind from a Category 1 hurricane blows out windows and rips off pieces of buildings. These objects become deadly flying debris. The storm can also topple trees and break power lines. A tree can fall on a person. It can crush a car or break through a roof. A downed power line can electrocute anyone who accidentally steps on it.

Hurricanes bring an even bigger danger from the sea. When a hurricane moves toward land, its winds

Hurricane winds can easily uproot trees.

push a huge amount of seawater in front of the storm. This rise in sea level is called a **storm surge**. A storm surge can span hundreds of miles across. When it comes ashore, it can travel miles inland. All that water can turn streets into rivers. Heavy objects floating in the water become dangerous battering rams. Cars, trees, street signs, telephone poles, and even boats can crash into buildings or people. Anything that breaks and floats

Hit at High Tide

The Great New England Hurricane of 1938 devastated the coasts of New York, Connecticut, Rhode Island, Massachusetts, and other areas of the Northeast. Its storm surge flooded the coast during a very high tide. The result was catastrophic. Rhode Island experienced a storm surge of 17 feet (5 m) above the normal tide level. Massachusetts recorded wave heights of 50 feet (15 m). Approximately 600 people were killed. Property damage totaled more than $600 million.

away becomes part of this deadly mass. Seawater also destroys underground electrical equipment. Thousands or even millions of people go without power for days or weeks at a time.

In some places, flash floods add to the danger. As the storm comes ashore and weakens, it releases its moisture as heavy rains. It is not uncommon for a few feet of rain to fall in a short period of time. Rivers and lakes can overflow their banks, flooding neighborhoods. People can become trapped in flooded homes.

HIGH TIDES AND STORM SURGES

Scientists have discovered that storm surges are even more dangerous if a hurricane hits at high tide. The tide is the constant change in sea level on shore lines. It is caused by the gravitational pull of the moon and sun on ocean water. High tide is the time of day when the water reaches its highest point.

A storm tide is the combination of the storm surge and the normal tide level. A 15-foot (4.5 m) storm surge combined with a 5-foot (1.5 m) high tide will produce a 20-foot (6 m) storm tide. Because a storm surge can affect hundreds of miles of coastline, the combination of the surge and the tide can cause major destruction.

Scientists use many tools to measure tides and surges. Tide stations are permanent structures where calm tides can be measured. High watermarks on trees and structures near the coast show how high tides and surges have risen in the past. Pressure sensors are placed on structures in the path of a hurricane as the storm approaches. They help scientists determine when water levels reach particular depths.

CHAPTER 5

MINIMIZING DAMAGE

In 2004, Hurricanes Charley, Frances, Gaston, Ivan, and Jeanne made landfall in the United States. These storms killed more than 60 people in the United States and caused more than $45 billion in damage. Hurricane Katrina hit in 2005, along with Dennis, Rita, and Wilma. The combined damage from these storms topped $110 billion, and thousands of lives were lost. These two hurricane seasons show the importance of protecting coastlines.

The failure of storm barriers led to flooding during Hurricanes Katrina and Sandy.

Governments, scientists, and **engineers** are looking at both "hard" and "soft" protection. Hard protections are made by people. Storm surge barriers, levees, and floodwalls separate coastal areas from the sea. Storm surge barriers and floodwalls are built with sturdy materials, such as concrete and steel. Some of these structures are more than 20 feet (6 m) high.

The structures include moving gates and walls. The walls remain open during good weather and close during a hurricane. Levees can occur naturally or be made by people. These raised ridges are usually made of packed earth and held together with vegetation. Manufactured barriers offer protection, but building and maintaining them costs millions of dollars. They can also damage wetlands, swamps, and barrier islands that are often part of a coastal community.

Soft protection is nature's way of protecting an area from flooding. It includes tangles of trees, grasses, and

Engineers try to work quickly to repair broken flood barriers.

other types of vegetation. These things help slow a surge. Protecting and restoring these natural barriers can give added protection.

Most scientists agree climate change is not the cause of any one hurricane, though its effects may make it easier for hurricanes to form and sustain themselves. Climate change will raise sea levels as polar ice melts, providing a bigger supply of water to power hurricanes. Some scientists think that over time this may produce bigger, more powerful storms.

The director of the National Weather Service, David Uccellini, spoke about higher sea levels after Typhoon Haiyan struck the Philippines in November 2013: "The fact that the sea levels are rising means that as you get these types of storm systems, you will be driving more water towards land."

Still, these changes will not necessarily make hurricanes more frequent in the near future. No hurricanes hit the United States in 2013. Meanwhile,

Scientists at the National Hurricane Center in Florida help warn people about coming hurricanes.

scientists and governments continue working to find better ways of protecting lives, land, and property. Better warning systems will help people prepare for hurricanes. Stronger barriers help minimize dangerous storm surges. These solutions will not remove all the risks. However, they do provide people with more time to avoid, survive, and prepare for these deadly storms.

CASE STUDY

IMPROVING DEFENSES AFTER KATRINA

Hurricane Katrina devastated New Orleans with a 10–19-foot (3–5.5 m) storm surge. More than 10 inches (25 cm) of rain fell in 24 hours. In some places, water reached more than 20 feet (6 m) high.

Much of the flooding happened because the flood protection system failed. Floodwaters damaged almost half of the protective structures in place. The water rose above or broke through 50 levees. To make matters worse, these structures prevented the water from draining away. Pumping the water out became difficult because more than 30 of 71 pumping stations were not working.

The US Army Corps of Engineers (USACE) is responsible for maintaining and building the city's flood defenses. After Hurricane Katrina, the organization looked at what went wrong. They found many outdated, weakened, and unfinished defenses.

Ever since then, the USACE has been building a new system. It includes higher and better-constructed levees, hundreds of miles of floodwalls and storm surge barriers, and the biggest water pumping station in the world.

Hurricane Isaac tested the new system in August 2012. It made landfall in southeastern Louisiana. The new defenses protected much of the New Orleans area from an almost 7-foot (2 m) storm surge.

TOP FIVE WORST HURRICANES

1. **The Great Hurricane of 1780**
   This monster storm killed about 22,000 people when it blasted Barbados, Martinique, St. Lucia, and other Caribbean islands. Such a large loss of life makes this storm the deadliest hurricane on record.

2. **Hurricane Mitch, 1998**
   Slow-moving Hurricane Mitch devastated Central America with its ferocious winds, heavy rainstorms, deadly mudslides, and severe flooding. With a death toll of more than 11,000 people, Hurricane Mitch is the second deadliest hurricane on record.

3. **Galveston Hurricane, 1900**
   With a 20-foot (6 m) storm surge and flash flooding, this hurricane literally drowned the city of Galveston, Texas. It took more than 6,000 lives, making it the deadliest hurricane to ever hit the United States.

4. **Hurricane Katrina, 2005**
   Hurricane Katrina ravaged New Orleans and other areas of the Gulf Coast. In New Orleans, floodwater covered more than 80 percent of the city. The hurricane killed more than 1,800 people.

5. **Florida Keys Labor Day Hurricane, 1935**
   This Category 5 storm is considered the strongest to hit the United States in the 1900s. It killed about 400 people.

LEARN MORE

FURTHER READING

Dougherty, Terri. *The Worst Hurricanes Of All Time*. North Mankato, MN: Capstone, 2012.

Jeffrey, Gary. *Hurricane Hunters & Tornado Chasers*. New York: Rosen, 2008.

Simon, Seymour. *Hurricanes*. New York: HarperCollins, 2007.

WEB SITES

National Geographic Kids—Hurricanes 101
http://video.nationalgeographic.com/video/kids/forces-of-nature-kids/hurricanes-101-kids
This Web site has a video that shows the destructive power of hurricanes. Three-dimensional computer graphics show how hurricanes form and cause damage.

Ready.gov—Hurricanes
http://www.ready.gov/kids/know-the-facts/hurricanes
This Web site features important information you can use to stay safe during a hurricane.

GLOSSARY

anemometers (an-i-MOM-uh-turs) instruments used to measure wind speed

barometers (buh-ROM-uh-turs) instruments that measure air pressure in the atmosphere

condenses (kuhn-DENSS-iz) turns from a gas into a liquid

dissipate (DISS-uh-payt) to break up and disappear

engineers (en-juh-NIHRS) people who use math and science to build things and solve problems

evacuation (i-vac-yooo-AY-shun) a movement of people out of a particular area

eye (EYE) a cloud-free area of light winds in the center of a hurricane

eyewall (EYE-wall) a violent wall of tall thunderstorms surrounding the eye and containing the heaviest rain and the strongest winds of the storm

humid (HYOO-mid) damp

rainbands (RAYN-bands) long bands of rain clouds that spiral in toward the eyewall

rain gauges (RAYN gayj-ez) instruments used to measure an amount of rainfall

satellites (SAT-uh-lites) objects that move in a curved path around a planet

storm surge (STORM surj) a huge rise in seawater produced by a hurricane's winds

telegraph (TEL-uh-graf) an early device used to send electronic signals through wires

INDEX